INSTANT MEMORIES™

Travel

READY-TO-USE SCRAPBOOK PAGES

Anna Corba

Sterling Publishing Co., Inc. New York
A Sterling/Chapelle Book

D1476343

Author: Anna Corba

If you have any questions or comments, please contact:
Chapelle, Ltd., Inc., P.O. Box 9252, Ogden, UT 84409
(801) 621-2777 • (801) 621-2788 Fax
e-mail: chapelle@chapelleltd.com
Web site: www.chapelleltd.com

Instant Memories is a trademark of Sterling Publishing Co., Inc.

PC Configuration: Windows 98 or later with 128 MB Ram or greater. At least 100 MB of free hard disk space. Dual speed or faster CD-ROM drive, and a 24-bit color monitor.

Macintosh Configuration: Mac OS 9 or later with 128 MB Ram or greater. At least 100 MB of free hard disk space. Dual speed or faster CD-ROM drive, and a 24-bit color monitor.

10 9 8 7 6 5 4 3 2 1

Published by Sterling Publishing Co., Inc.
387 Park Avenue South, New York, NY 10016
© 2005 by Sterling Publishing Co., Inc.
Distributed in Canada by Sterling Publishing
c/o Canadian Manda Group, 165 Dufferin Street
Toronto, Ontario, Canada M6K 3H6
Distributed in Great Britain by Chrysalis Books Group PLC,
The Chrysalis Building, Bramley Road, London W10 6SP, England
Distributed in Australia by Capricorn Link (Australia) Pty. Ltd.
P. O. Box 704, Windsor, NSW 2756, Australia
Printed and Bound in China
All Rights Reserved

Sterling ISBN 1-4027-2643-0

For information about custom editions, special sales, premium and corporate purchases, please contact Sterling Special Sales Department at 800-805-5489 or specialsales@sterlingpub.com.

Introduction

Scrapbooking is a wonderful way to document holidays, celebrations, special day-to-day events, and family history. However, not everyone has the time or the money to do what it takes to create show-stopping scrapbook pages. That's where the *Instant Memories™ Ready-to-Use Scrapbook Page* series comes in. The top designers in the field have done all the work for you; simply add your favorite photos to their layouts and you're done! Or add a few embellishments such as a charm or ribbon and you have a unique personalized page in minutes. You can tear the pages directly from the book, photocopy them to use time and again, or print them from the enclosed CD.

As an added bonus in the *Instant Memories* series, we have included hundreds of rare vintage images on the enclosed CD-rom. From Victorian postcards to hand-painted beautiful borders and frames, it would take years to acquire a collection like this. However, with this easy-to-use resource, you'll have them all right here, right now, to use for any computer project over and again. Each image has been reproduced to the highest quality standard for photocopying and scanning and can be reduced or enlarged to suit your needs.

Perfect for paper crafting, scrapbooking, and fabric transfers, *Instant Memories* books will inspire you to explore new avenues of creativity. We've included a sampling of ideas to get you started, but the best part is using your imagination to create your own projects. Be sure to look for other books in this series as we continue to search the markets for wonderful vintage images.

How to Use This Book

General Instructions:

The art pages in this book are printed on one side only, making it easy to simply tear out the pages and use as is; or if you choose, you can cut out individual images to use on our own pages and projects. However, you'll probably want to use them again, so the enclosed CD-Rom contains all of the images individually as well as in the page layout form. The images are large enough to use at 12" x 12". The CDs can be used with both PC and Mac formats. Just pop in the disk. On a PC, the file will immediately open to the Home page, which will walk you through how to view and print the images. For Macintosh users, you will simply double-click on the icon to open. The images may also be incorporated into your computer projects using simple imaging software that you can purchase specifically for this purpose—a perfect choice for digital scrapbooking.

The reference numbers printed on the back of each image in the book are the same ones used on the CD, which will allow you to easily find the image you are looking for. The numbering consists of the book abbreviation, the page number, the image number, and the file format. The first file number (located next to the page number) is for the entire page. For example, TRA01-01.jpg would be the entire image for page 1 of Travel. The second file number is for the top-right image. The numbers continue in a counterclockwise circular fashion.

Once you have resized your images, added text, created a scrapbook page, etc., you are ready to print them. Printing on cream or white cardstock, particularly a textured variety, creates a more authentic look. You won't be able to tell that it's a reproduction! If you don't have access to a computer or printer, that's ok. Most photocopy centers can resize and print your images for a nominal fee, or they have do-it-yourself machines that are easy to use.

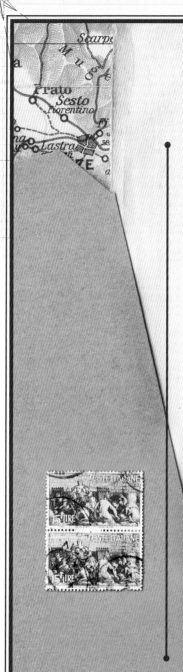

Ideas for Using the Images:

Scrapbooking: These images are perfect for both heritage and modern scrapbook pages. Simply use the image as a frame, accent piece, or border. For those of you with limited time, the page layouts in this book have been created so that you can use them as they are. Simply print out or photocopy the desired page, attach a photograph into one of the boxes, add your own journaling, and you have a beautiful designer scrapbook page in minutes. Be sure to print your images onto acid-free cardstock so the pages will last a lifetime.

Cards: Some computer programs allow images to be inserted into a card template, simplifying cardmaking. If this is not an option, simply use the images as accent pieces on the front or inside of the card. Use a bone folder to score the card's fold to create a more professional look.

Decoupage/Collage Projects: For decoupage or collage projects, photocopy or print the image onto a thinner paper such as copier paper. Thin paper adheres to projects more effectively. Decoupage medium glues and seals the project, creating a gloss or matte finish when dry, thus protecting the image. Vintage images are beautiful when decoupaged to cigar boxes, glass plates, and even wooden plaques. The possibilities are endless.

Fabric Arts: Vintage images can be used in just about any fabric craft imaginable: wall hangings, quilts, bags, or baby bibs. Either transfer the image onto the fabric by using a special iron-on paper, or by printing the image directly onto the fabric, using a temporary iron-on stabilizer that stabilizes the fabric to feed through a printer. These items are available at most craft and sewing stores. If the item will be washed, it is better to print directly on the fabric. For either method, follow the instructions on the package.

Wood Transfers: It is now possible to print images on wood. Use this exciting technique to create vintage plaques, clocks, frames, and more. A simple, inexpensive transfer tool is available at most large craft or home improvement stores, or online from various manufacturers. You simply place the photocopy of the image you want, face down, onto the surface and use the tool to transfer the image onto the wood. This process requires a copy from a laser printer, which means you will probably have to get your copies made at a copy center. Refer to manufacturer's instructions for additional details. There are other transfer products available that can be used with wood. Choose the one that is easiest for you.

Gallery of Ideas

These *Travel* images can be used in a variety of projects—cards, scrapbook pages, and decoupage projects to name a few. The images can be used as they are shown in the layout, or you can copy and clip out individual images, or portions or multitudes of images. The following pages contain a collection of ideas to inspire you to use your imagination and create one-of-a-kind treasures.

Idea 1

This page was easily personalized by adding a favorite photograph, a few rubber-stamped images, and several appropriate postage stamps.

Art Page 14

Idea 2 A snippet of ribbon, a photograph, and some personal journaling were all that was needed to finish this fabulous page.

Art Page 15

Idea 3 Just because a picture appears on an art page doesn't mean you have to use it. Simply cover it with a photo of choice, as was done here.

Art Page 56

Art Page 57

Idea 4

Buttons are a wonderful addition to scrapbook pages. Try sewing them on with thread, rather than gluing.

Idea 5 Postage cancellation stamps are fun to use on your travel pages. You can often find these stamps at antiques stores or flea markets.

Art Page 29

Art Page 28

Idea 6 The blank postcard on the art page is the perfect spot for journaling and for adding a colorful photograph. Postage stamps and a rubber-stamped title complete the page.

Idea 7 Tiny shells add a delicate touch to this seaside page. Place heavy page protectors between pages with dimensional items to prevent indentations.

Art Page 53

Idea 8 Journaling tells a story on this page, while bright photographs show it. Sheer ribbon adds delicate color and dimension.

Art Page 52

Idea 9

This art page was used to set the tone for an entire album. Game tiles and a checkered ribbon add a touch of whimsy to this vintage cover.

Art Page 47

... redevable du grand succès de cette ... u génie français.

... recteur des finances de l'Exposition. ... administration, M. Grison s'est élevé ... ... aux plus hauts degrés de la hiérarchie, après s'être distingué, en maintes occasions, notamment dans le règlement des comptes de l'Exposition de 1878, ainsi que dans les liquidations des comptes d'approvisionnements faits pendant le siège en 1870. M. Grison était directeur de la comptabilité au Ministère du Commerce, lorsqu'il fut chargé de la mission de diriger le service des finances à l'Exposition.

MOYENS DE TRANSPORT

Les moyens de transport pour se rendre à l'Exposition sont nombreux. Il en existe de tous genres : voitures, chemin de fer, bateaux, omnibus et tramways.

CHEMIN DE FER

Le chemin de fer de l'Ouest a, au Champ de Mars, un ...branchement spécial, auquel on peut se rendre de la gare ... ...bord et ensuite d'Asnières, d'Argenteuil, de ... ... la Ceinture.

A Map of an Estate of Captain IOHN BARKER lying in the parishes of Barsesla & Stradbrook in the County of Suffolk which Contain as in the Table of Contents.

REPUBLICA ARGENTINA
M.J.I.
10c

CARTE POSTALE
REPUBLIQUE FRANÇAISE
15c
Cartes "La Cigogne", 17, Rue Jules Cours, Rouen

Mrs. Formley
Archer Av.
Mount Vernon
New York
U.S.A.

Seeing Toronto in the Tourist Car.
KING

6/24/09

TRA01-04

TRA01-03

TRA01-02

TRA01-05

TRA01-06

TRA01-08

TRA01-07

1 — TRA01-01

TRA02-03

TRA02-02

TRA02-04

TRA02-06

TRA02-05

TRA02-01 | 2

Palermo - Villa Igiea.

Palermo - Monte Pellegrino visto dal mare.

HOTEL
LUNA
VENEZIA

VIAREGGIO
Scala di 1 : 17.000

TRA03-03

TRA03-02

TRA03-04

TRA03-05

TRA03-07

TRA03-06

3 — TRA03-01

TRA04-03

TRA04-02

TRA04-04

TRA04-07

TRA04-06

TRA04-05

TRA04-01 | 4

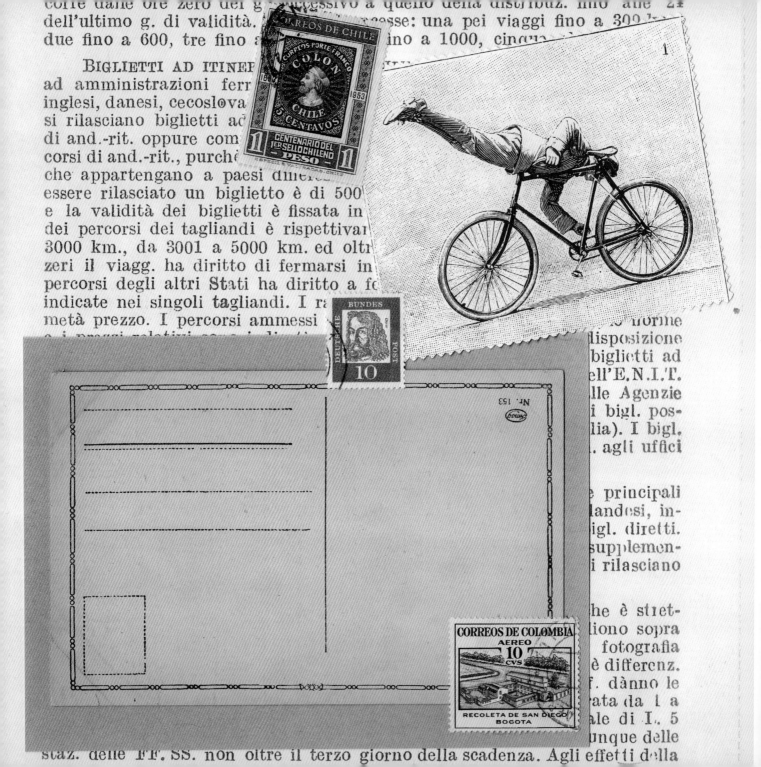

corre dalle ore zero dei g. ... essivo a quello della distribuz. fino alle 24
dell'ultimo g. di validità. ... resse: una pei viaggi fino a 300 k...
due fino a 600, tre fino a ... fino a 1000, cinque ...

BIGLIETTI AD ITINE...
ad amministrazioni ferr...
inglesi, danesi, cecoslova...
si rilasciano biglietti ad...
di and.-rit. oppure com...
corsi di and.-rit., purché...
che appartengano a paesi dive...
essere rilasciato un biglietto è di 500...
e la validità dei biglietti è fissata in...
dei percorsi dei tagliandi è rispettivam...
3000 km., da 3001 a 5000 km. ed oltr...
zeri il viagg. ha diritto di fermarsi in...
percorsi degli altri Stati ha diritto a f...
indicate nei singoli tagliandi. I ra...
metà prezzo. I percorsi ammessi ... ...o norme
... i prezzi relativi sono indica... ...isposizione
... biglietti ad
... ...ell'E.N.I.T.
... ...lle Agenzie
... i bigl. pos-
... ...lia). I bigl.
... ... agli uffici

... e principali
... ...landesi, in-
... ...igl. diretti.
... ...supplemen-
... i rilasciano

... ...he è stret-
... ...iono sopra
... ... fotografia
... è differenz.
... f. dànno le
... ...ata da 1 a
... ...ale di L. 5
... ...unque delle
staz. delle FF. SS. non oltre il terzo giorno della scadenza. Agli effetti della

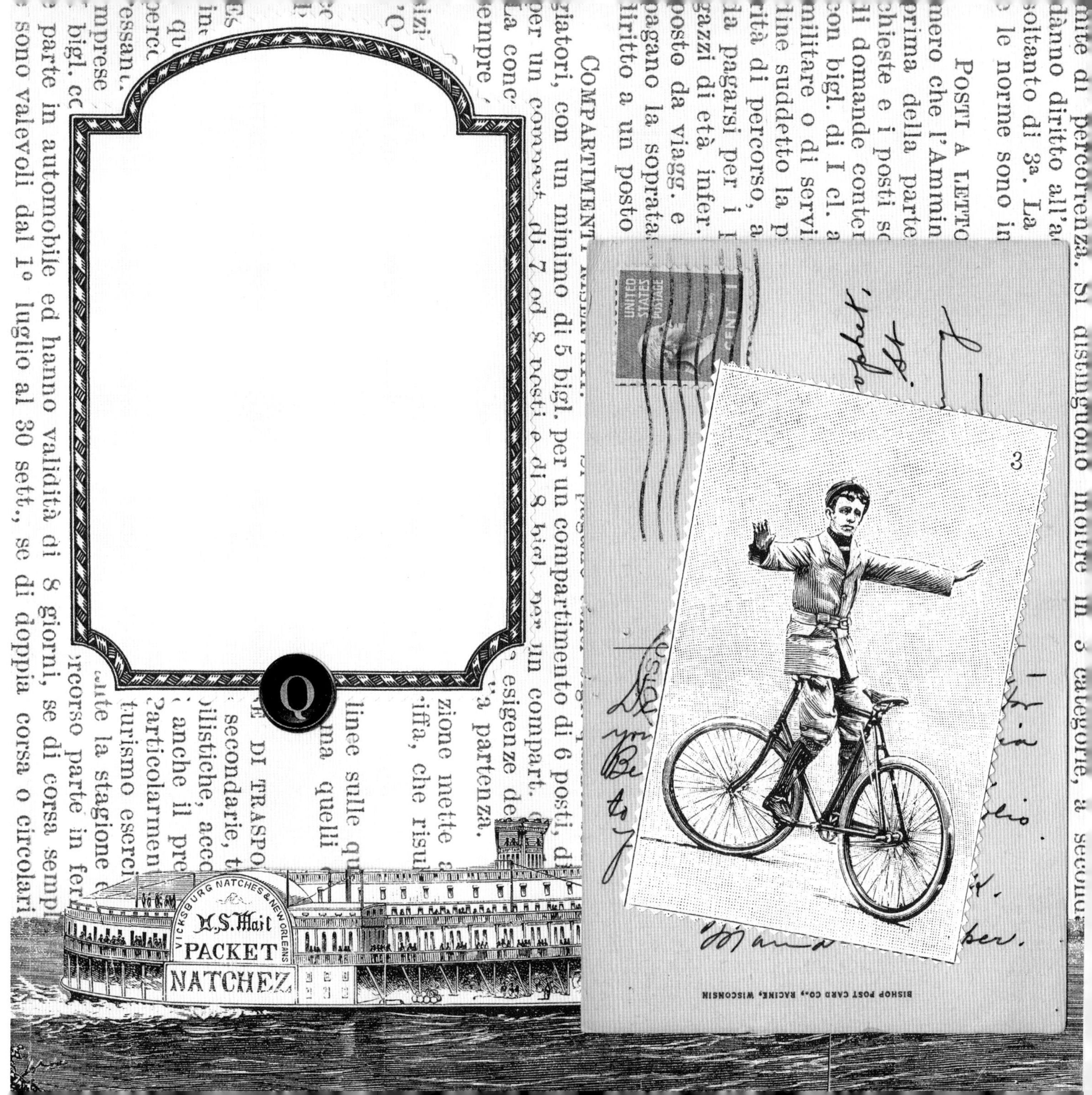

Q
VICKSBURG NATCHES & NEW ORLEANS
U.S. Mail
PACKET
NATCHEZ
3

TRA05-03

TRA05-02

TRA05-04

TRA05-05

TRA05-06

5 — TRA05-01

TRA06-03

TRA06-02

TRA06-09

TRA06-04

TRA06-08

TRA06-05

TRA06-07

TRA06-06

TRA06-01 — 6

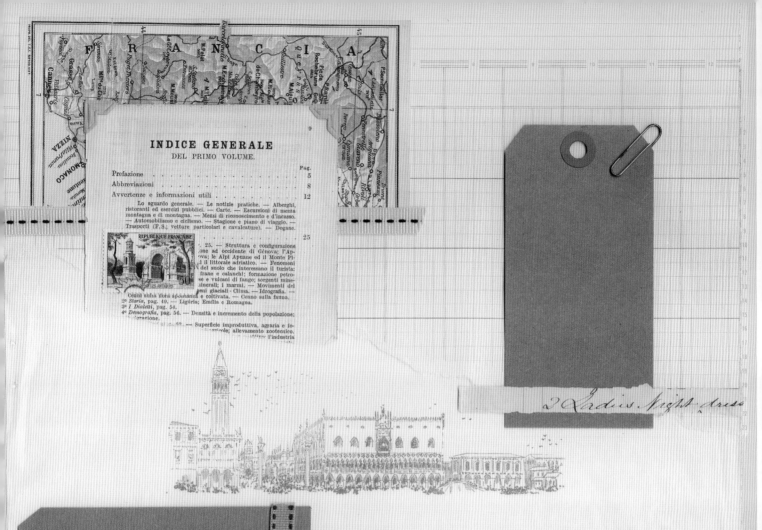

FRANCIA

25. — Struttura e configurazione ... one ad occidente di Génova; l'Ap... nova; le Alpi Apuane ed il Monte Pi... il littorale adriatico. — Fenomeni ... del suolo che interessano il turista: ... frane e calanchi; formazione petro... se e vulcani di fango; sorgenti mine... minerali; i marmi. — Movimenti del ...eni glaciali - Clima. — Idrografia. — Cenni sulla flora spontanea e coltivata. — Cenno sulla fauna.
2° *Storia*, pag. 49. — Ligùria; Emilia e Romagna.
3° *I Dialetti*, pag. 54.
4° *Demografia*, pag. 56. — Densità e incremento della popolazione; ...grazione.
...° ...— Superficie improduttiva, agraria e fo-... ...one; allevamento zootecnico. ...tivo l'industria

2 Ladies Night dress

VENISE

Et les palais antiques,
Et les graves portiques,
Et les blancs escaliers
    Des chevaliers,

Et les ponts et les rues,
Et les mornes statues,
Et le golfe mouvant
    Qui tremble au vent,

Tout se tait, fors les gardes
Aux longues hallebardes,
Qui veillent aux créneaux
    Des arsenaux.

Autour de lui, par groupes,
Navires et chaloupes,
Pareils à des hérons
    Couchés en ronds,

Dorment sur l'eau qui fume,
Et croisent dans la brume,
En légers tourbillons,

Sur sa couche embaumée,
La Vanina pâmée
Presse encor son amant,
    En s'endormant;

Et Narcisa, la folle,
Au fond de sa gondole,
S'oublie en un festin
    Jusqu'au matin.

Et qui, dans l'Italie,
N'a son grain de folie?
Qui ne garde aux amours
    Ses plus beaux jours?

Laissons la vieille horloge,
Au palais du vieux doge,
Lui compter de ses nuits

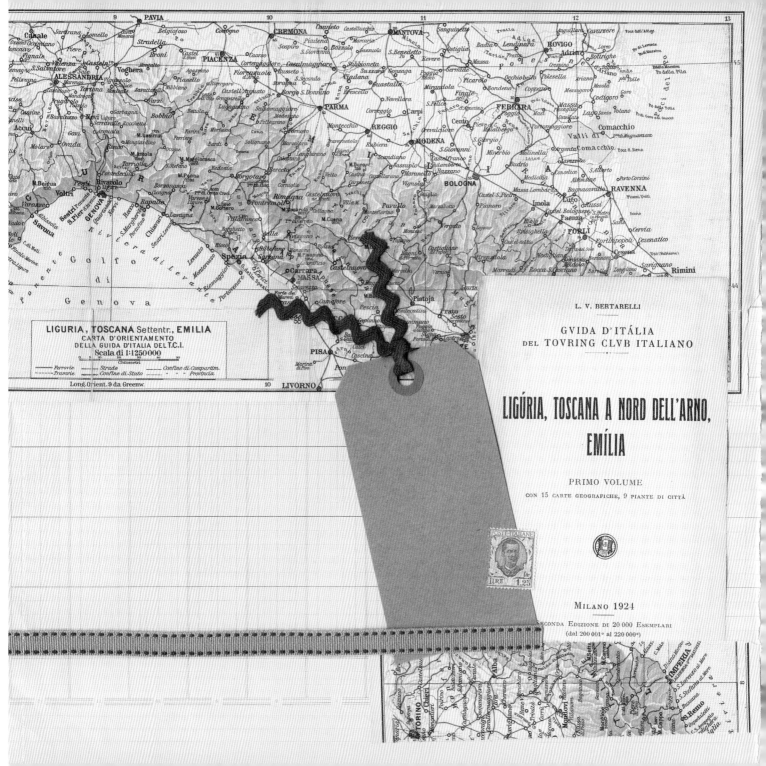

TRA07-02

TRA07-03

TRA07-07

TRA07-06

TRA07-04

TRA07-05

7 — TRA07-01

TRA08-03

TRA08-02

TRA08-04

TRA08-05

TRA08-09

TRA08-06

TRA08-07

TRA08-01 | 8

TRA08-08

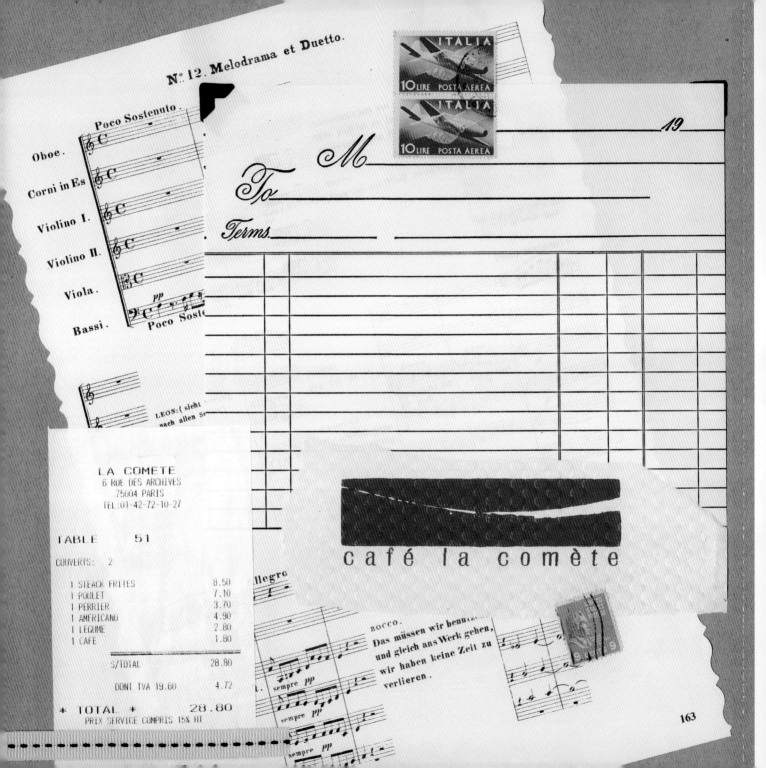

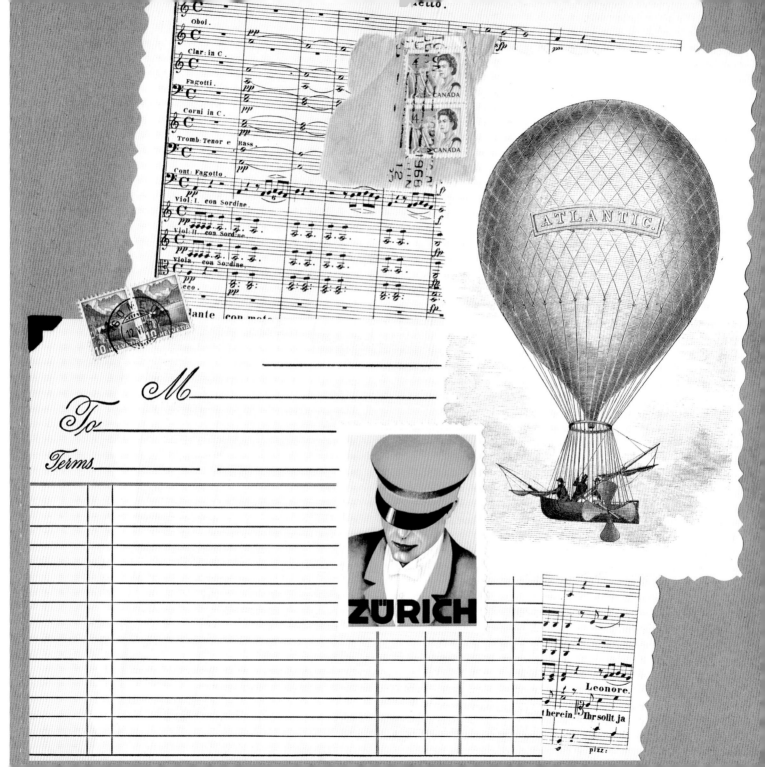

TRA09-02

TRA09-03

TRA09-04

TRA09-07

TRA09-06

TRA09-05

9 — | TRA09-01 |

TRA10-02

TRA10-03

TRA10-06

TRA10-07

TRA10-05

TRA10-04

TRA10-01 | 10

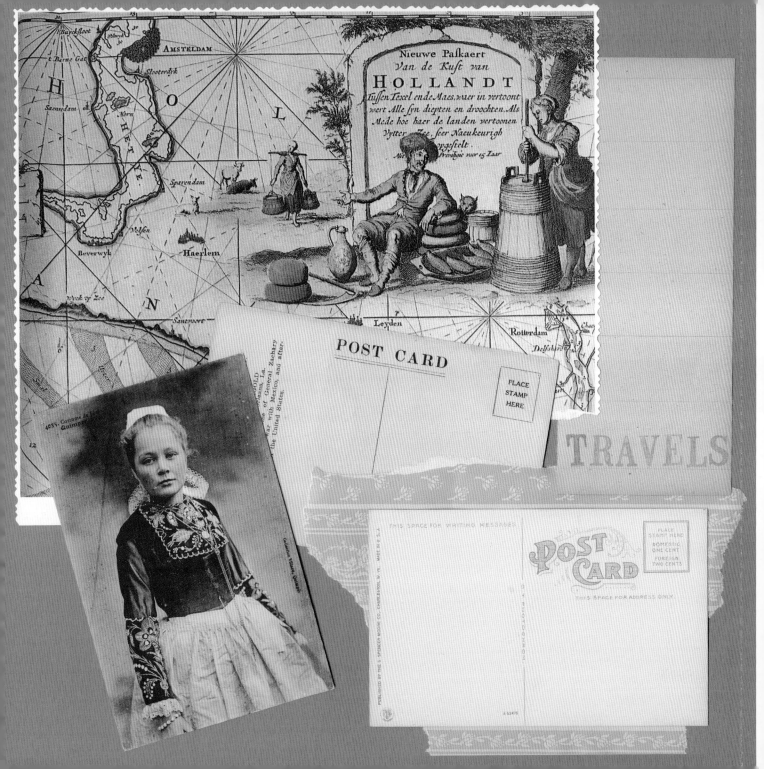

Nieuwe Paſkaert
Van de Kuſt van
HOLLANDT
Tuſſen Texel en de Maes, waer in vertoont
wert Alle ſyn diepten en droochten. Als
Mede hoe haer de landen vertoonen
Uytter Zee, ſeer Naeukeurigh
op'gheſtelt.

POST CARD

PLACE
STAMP
HERE

TRAVELS

THIS SPACE FOR WRITING MESSAGES

PLACE
STAMP HERE
DOMESTIC
ONE CENT
FOREIGN
TWO CENTS

POST
CARD

THIS SPACE FOR ADDRESS ONLY

Den Haag. Mauritshuis

TOMBOLA TOMBOLA **TOMBOLA**

801 801 801

TALON | Ce coupon peut être plié et placé dans une corbeille pour le tirage | A conserver par le Souscripteur

POST CARD

FAMOUS SUPERIOR QUALITY THROUGHOUT THE WORLD

Address Only

Postkarte
CARTE POSTALE — POST CARD.

(Nur für die Adresse).

Familie
Simon-Pierre
Caffe-Restaurant
Luxembourg
Bonnaweg Nr. 29

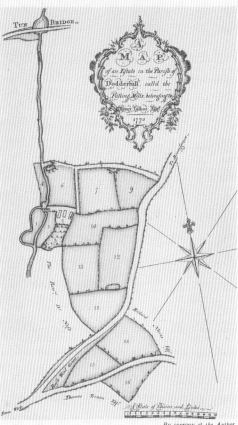

TUN BRIDGE

A MAP of an Estate in the Parish of Dodderhill called the Fulling Mills, belonging to Henry Talbot Esq. 1770

By courtesy of the Author

THE ESTATE OF CHARLES HENRY TALBOT, DODDERHILL, 1770
Typical MS. Estate Map of the Eighteenth Century

TRA11-03

TRA11-02

TRA11-06

TRA11-07

TRA11-04

TRA11-05

11 — TRA11-01

TRA12-02

TRA12-03

TRA12-05

TRA12-04

TRA12-01   12

LUNEDI MONDAY LUNDI MONTAG ПОНЕДЕЛЬНИК 月	MARTEDI TUESDAY MARDI DIENSTAG ВТОРНИК 火	MERCOLEDI WEDNESDAY MERCREDI MITTWOCH СРЕДА 水	GIOVEDI THURSDAY JEUDI DONNERSTAG ЧЕТВЕРГ 木	VENERDI FRIDAY VENDREDI FREITAG ПЯТНИЦА 金	SABATO SATURDAY SAMEDI SAMSTAG СУББОТА 土
1	2	3	4	5	6
8	9	10	11		
15	16	17	18		

BISCUITS -:- CHOCOLAT -:- CONFISERIE -:- DRAGÉES

· J. MOREAU ·

TÉLÉPHONE — 104 —

MAISON DE VENTE : 7, Rue du Temple
USINE ET BUREAUX à Saint-Amatre —

CHÈQUES POSTAUX
Compte Paris
Saint-Roch. n° 9527

AUXERRE, LE -6 FEV 1925 192

Monsieur Michaut Ancy. Doit

RELEVÉ DE COMPTE

Com. Auxerre 446.

MA FACTURE

Timbre

Les Réclamations doivent
être adressées dans les 48 heures

Valeur en ma traite au FIN COURANT sauf versement de
votre part à mon compte-courant de chèques postaux d'ici QUINZE COURANT

BANQUE DE FRANCE
DIX FRANCS
LE CAISSIER PRINCIPAL   LE SECRÉTAIRE GÉNÉRAL

189

TRA13-02

TRA13-03

TRA13-06

TRA13-04

TRA13-05

13 — TRA13-01

TRA14-02

TRA14-03

TRA14-04

TRA14-06

TRA14-05

TRA14-01　14

La Princesse en croupe se met,
Sans prendre congé de son hôte.
L'inconnu, qui pour quelque temps
S'était défait de tous ses gens,
Les rencontra bientôt. Il avait dans sa troupe
Un sien neveu fort jeune, avec son Gouverneur.
Notre héroïne prend, en descendant de croupe,
Un palefroi. Cependant le Seigneur
Marche toujours à côté d'elle,
Tantôt lui conte une nouvelle,
Et tantôt lui parle d'amour,
Pour rendre le chemin plus court.

Avec beaucoup de foi le traité s'exécute.
Pas la moindre ombre de dispute :
Point de faute au calcul, non plus qu'entre marchands.

Le _____

Table N° _____ **Total Prix Net** _____

22   dont TVA à _____ %

_____

Table N° _____

22

TOTAL SERVICE COMPRIS _____

TRA15-02

TRA15-07 TRA15-06

TRA15-03

TRA15-05

15 — TRA15-01

TRA15-04

TRA16-02

TRA16-03

TRA16-10

TRA16-09

TRA16-08

TRA16-04

TRA16-07

TRA16-06

TRA16-05

TRA16-01 **16**

PLAN DE L'EXPOSITION UNIVERSELLE INTERNATIONALE DE 1889

CHEMIN DE FER

dans l'extension de l'exposition

allant du quai d'Orsay à l'École militaire

ALLER ET RETOUR

A   Station de départ (quai d'Orsay)
B   Halte Halle
C   Halte d'Iéna
D   Station d'Iéna
E   Halte Diane (École militaire)
F   Station d'arrivée

SEINE

FLEUVE

Restaurants
Brasseries
W.C

9

SOCIÉTÉ NATIONALE DES CHEMINS DE FER FRANÇAIS

N° 169

Ongle... ...le
po... ...le
1/2 tarif enfant

148348

ARRAS — PARIS-NORD 369

TICKET

INDIANA TICKET CO.

E. V. 124. PARIS. — Gare du Nord et Boulevard Denain

— 169 —

BUREAUX CORRESPONDANT
AVEC CES LIGNES

Square Montholon.
Rue de Châteaudun.
Place de la Trinité.
Gare Saint-Lazare.
Boulevard Malesherbes.
Saint-Philippe-du-Roule.
Champs-Élysées.
Palais-Royal.
Place Saint-Pierre.

LIGNES CONDUISANT
A L'EXPOSITION

Gare de l'Est
au
Trocadéro

Porte Saint-Martin
à
Grenelle

Gare de Lyon
au
Pont de l'Alma

La Villette
au
Trocadéro

Louvre
à
Passy

Louvre
à
Saint-Cloud

Louvre

O   U   I

D'en avoir soin ? si n'est on mis en peine
Quand, malgré moi, l'on m'a jointe avec vous :
Vous, vieux penard ; moi, fille jeune et drue,
Qui méritais d'être un peu mieux pourvue
Et de goûter ce qu'hymen a de doux ?
Pour cet effet j'étais ass
Et me trouvais aussi
De ces plaisirs, que j'
Or est le cas allé d'aut
J'ai pris mari qui pour
N'a jamais eu que ses jo
Mais Pagamin, sitôt qu'i
Me sut donner bien une a
J'ai plus appris des choses
Depuis deux jours qu'en q
Laissez-moi donc, Monsieur
Sur mon retour n'insistez da
Calendriers ne sont point en
Chez Pagamin, je vous en av

CARTE POSTALE

Ce côté est exclusivement réservé à l'adresse

M

LANGAGE DES TIMBRES

Joie et Bonheur

Mes pensées pour vous

Je pense à vous

Sincère Amour

Je vous aime

doux Baisers

67395106 02   67395106
Transports en Île-de-France   Transports en Île-de-France

— 253 —

PARC MONTSOURIS

Situé boulevard Jourdan, le parc de Montsouris, vaste
et accidenté, fut aménagé en 1878. On y remarque le monu-
ment élevé à la mémoire du colonel Flatters, le Bardo
ou palais du bey de Tunis.

Il existe, au parc Montsouris, un observatoire où se font
les différentes études climatologiques et météorologiques.

Le parc est ouvert au public, tous les jours, de 6 heures du
matin à 10 heures du soir.

ÉGLISES DE PARIS

Notre-Dame, cathédrale de Paris, visible tous les jours
de neuf heures à six heures. — Les tours ont 70 mètres de
hauteur et la flèche 130 mètres ; en payant 25 centimes,
on peut visiter le bourdon. — Le portail de Notre-Dame
est un chef-d'œuvre de sculpture.

Notre-Dame fut construite sous Philippe Auguste ; elle
    ogival. A l'intérieur, les nefs, les chapelles, les
   x, le grand orgue forment un ensemble ab-
   ose et merveilleux.
   renferme les tombeaux des archevêques, et les
   is XIII et Louis XV.
   ine, située à l'extrémité de la rue Royale, face
    la Concorde, est une des plus belles églises de
   fut commencée sous le règne de Louis XV, en
   l'architecte Vignon (style grec).
   Eustache, à la pointe de ce nom. — Angle des
   ontmartre et Rambuteau. Entrée principale : rue du
   Construite au dix-septième siècle (en 1645) ; — style
   ssance. Cette église, très vaste, aux voûtes très élevées,

15

CARTE POSTALE

Paris réimprimée à la Correspondance

Mademoiselle
Madeleine Sennefs

Bord bordel
Nancy

Mademoiselle
Madeleine Sennefs
155 rue de Curné
Sud

Monsieur Pierre Rabé
à Peyrondine (Monget)
par Samadet
Landes

TRA17-03

TRA17-02

TRA17-04

TRA17-05

TRA17-10

TRA17-09

TRA17-06

TRA17-08

TRA17-07

17 — TRA17-01

TRA18-02

TRA18-03

TRA18-04

TRA18-07

TRA18-06

TRA18-05

| TRA18-01 | 18 |

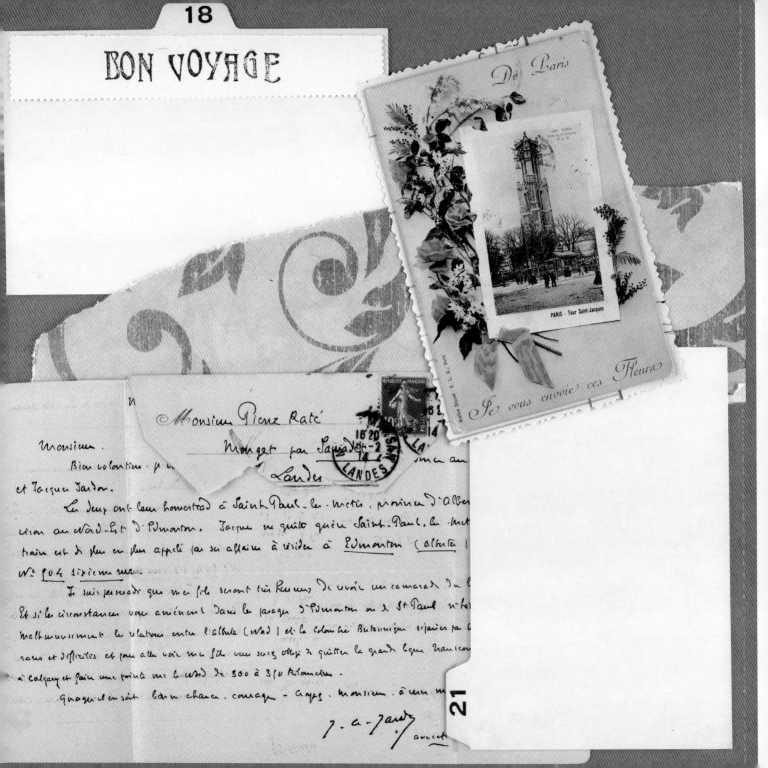

BON VOYAGE

18

De Paris

PARIS - Tour Saint-Jacques

Je vous envoie ces Fleurs

Monsieur Pierre Raté

Monget par Samadet

Landes

Monsieur,

Bien volontiers je

et Jacques Jardon.

Les deux ont leur homestead à Saint-Paul-les-Métis, province d'Alberta

vion au Nord-Est d'Edmonton. Jacques ne quitte guère Saint-Paul-les-Métis

train est de plus en plus appelé par ses affaires à visiter à Edmonton (Alberta)

N° 904 sixième rue.

Je suis persuadé que mes fils seront très heureux de revoir un camarade du

Et si les circonstances vous amènent dans les parages d'Edmonton ou de St-Paul, n'hé

malheureusement les relations entre l'Alberta (Nord) et la Colombie Britannique séparées par l

rares et difficiles et pour aller voir mon fils vous serez obligé de quitter le grand ligne transcon

à Calgary et faire une pointe vers le nord de 300 à 350 kilomètres.

Quoiqu'il en soit bonne chance, courage — Croyez, Monsieur, à mes m

J. A. Jardon

21

CARTE POSTALE

CORRESPONDANCE   ADRESSE

Chère cousine   faute moi je nai
je t'écrit ses deux   pas le temps moi
mots pour te dire   je te ferais autre
si tu veux me faire   chose quand tu
un bas de pantalon et   pourra cela me ferais
un non mièsement de   bien plaisir je te quitte
chemise tu se vais bien   en vous vous embrassent
                                 de cœur et d'amitier

15

TRA19-03   TRA19-02

TRA19-04

TRA19-05

                                              TRA19-07

TRA19-06

19─| TRA19-01 |

TRA20-03   TRA20-02

TRA20-04

TRA20-05   TRA20-08

TRA20-07

TRA20-06

TRA20-01   20

CONTES DE LA FONTAINE

84

Qui se mourait pour vous d'amour ;
Vous jeûnerez à votre tour,
Ou vous me serez favorable.
La justice le veut : nous autres gens de mer

vez-moi. »

faire ;
là,
rème :

?
ut.

dre,
ons,

POST CARD

THIS SIDE FOR THE ADDRESS

20-1-22.

Ma chère Marthe,

J'ai appris par mon frère Gustave, enfin, le montant de ce que vous estimez que je vous dois. Mais comme il vous a été répondu je suis seule chargée de vous régler. J'ai passé l'âge d'avoir un tuteur aussi je prie par le même courrier mon frère Pierre qui tous les mois me règle l'héritage de ma mère vous faire parvenir 50. pendant 4 mois, soit

RÉPUBLIQUE FRANÇAISE

TRA21-02

TRA21-03

TRA21-08

TRA21-04

TRA21-05

TRA21-07

21 — TRA21-01

TRA21-06

TRA22-04   TRA22-03   TRA22-02

TRA22-05

                                          TRA22-08

                              TRA22-07

        TRA22-06

                                        TRA22-01 22

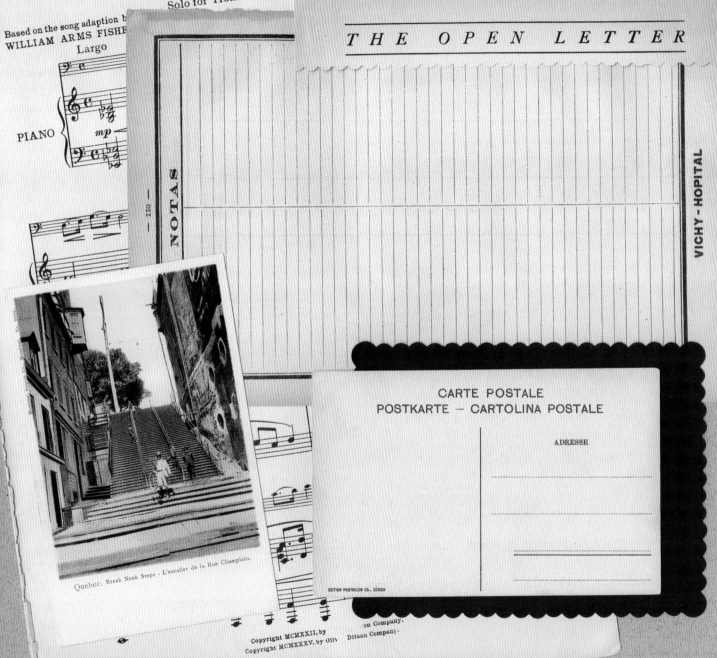

A los enfermos que no les sea posible adquirir las aguas minerales de **VICHY-ÉTAT**, embotelladas en Vichy (Francia) con todos los cuidados indispensables, y que son las únicas que tan maravillosos resultados producen tomadas a domicilio, pueden, en su defecto, (con agua hervida y enfriada) **preparar por sí mismos** una excelente solución alcalina, altamente digestiva y diurética, la que además de facilitar la digestión, limpia el hígado y los intestinos, **y disuelve y elimina el ácido úrico**, empleando la

SAL
VICHY-ÉTAT

VICHY · ÉTAT

SEL NATUREL
POUR
BOISSON

IN OLD MADRID.

Solo for Trombone (or Baritone)

H. TROTÈRE.
arr. by T. H. Rollinson.

29

ROMA - Il Vaticano

PER VIA AEREA
PAR AVION

Copyright MCMXI by Oliver Ditson Company

TRA23-03

TRA23-02

TRA23-04

TRA23-07

TRA23-05

TRA23-06

23 — TRA23-01

TRA24-03   TRA24-02

TRA24-04

TRA24-08

TRA24-05

TRA24-07

TRA24-06

TRA24-01 24

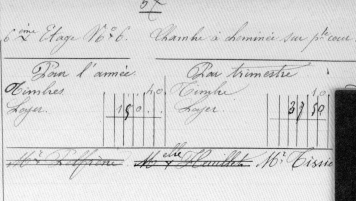

57

6° Etage N° 6. Chambre à cheminée sur p^te cour.

	Pour l'année				Par trimestre			
Timbres.			40		Timbre			10
Loyer.	150				Loyer	37	50	

Mr Delfrène   M^r & Houillet   Mr Tissie

THE CHÂTEAUX OF THE LOIRE

Between Gien and Angers the banks of the Loire and the valleys of its tributaries offer an ... châteaux or country mansions ... and history and they occupy ... quiet lines, owes its charm to ... e skies, long stretches of often ... y slopes with fertile vineyards, ... enes. It is a restful landscape, ... were built in the Renaissance ... u. Blois, Chambord, Chau- ... r, the castles of ... 05 ... ges, and

dant le reste du voyage.
Soudan (2) il la présenta.
imer ici la tendresse,
mieux dire, les transports
en voyant la Princesse,
de nouveaux efforts,
faire : il est bon que j'imite
sur la fin du jour
dinaire si court,
qu'il se précipite.
à se faire écouter ;
rincesse.

20 CARTES POSTALES ILLUSTRÉES DÉTACHABLES

Monte-Carlo

PHOTO-CAUVIN - NICE

Le Diner

2

Collection Artistique
725 bis. - MONTE-CARLO. - Casino et Jardins

60

6ᵉ Étage N° 9.

Cabinet sur 9ᵉ cour.

RESTAURANT
COCONNAS

37 gr.

Total
Carbohydrates
50.7 gr.

TRA25-03　　　　　　　　　　TRA25-02

TRA25-04

TRA25-07

TRA25-05

TRA25-06

25─| TRA25-01 |

TRA26-02

TRA26-03

TRA26-04

TRA26-10

TRA26-05

TRA26-09

TRA26-06

TRA26-08

TRA26-01   26

TRA26-07

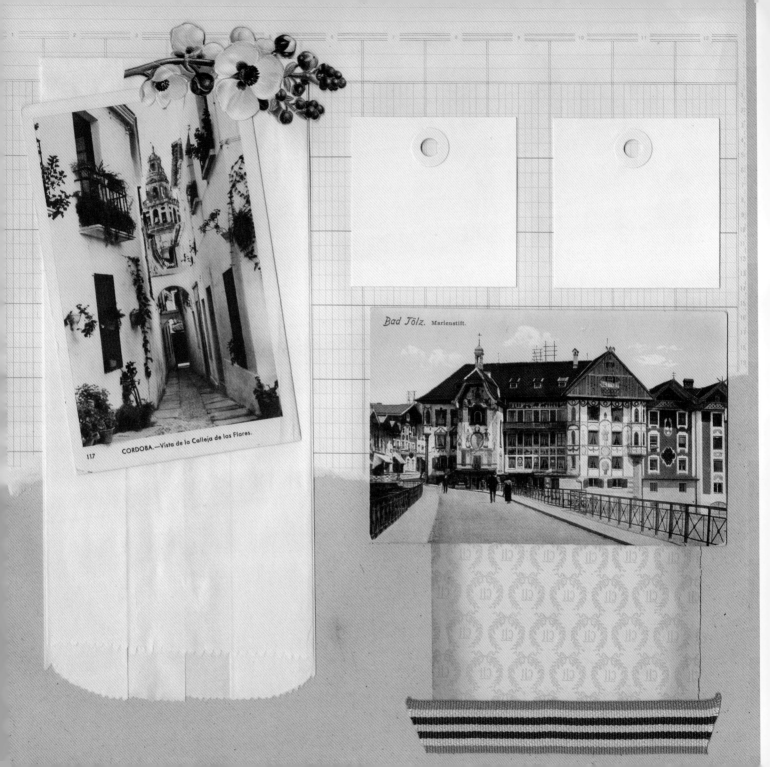

CORDOBA.—Vista de la Calleja de las Flores.

117

Bad Tölz. Marienstift.

CENTRAL

	JAN.	FEB.	MAR.	APR.	MAY	JUNE	JULY	AUG.	SEPT.	OCT.	NOV.	DEC.
Chicago	25°	27°	36°	47°	58°	68°	73°	72°	65°	54°	40°	30°
Lat. N41°52'—Alt. 595'	11*	10*	12*	11	12	11	9	9	10*	11		
Cincinnati	33°	34°	43°	54°	64°	73°	77°	75°	69°	57°	45°	3
Lat. N39°06'—Alt. 550'	13*	12*	13*	12	12	11	10	9	8	8	10	11
Cleveland	25°	26°	35°	46°	58°	68°	72°	70°	64°	53°	39°	2
Lat. N41°29'—Alt. 580'	17	15	15	13	13	11	10	9	10	11	14	1
Dallas	45°	50°	57°	65°	73°	81°	84°	84°	78°	68°	56°	4
Lat. N32°47'—Alt. 435'	8*	8*	8*	8*	9	7	5	7	5	6	6	
Detroit	25°	25°	34°	46°	58°	68°	73°	71°	64°	53°	40°	2
Lat. N42°19'—Alt. 585'	13*	12*	13*	11*	13	11	9	9	10	10	12*	1
Minneapolis	14°	17°	30°	46°	58°	68°	73°	71°	62°	50°	33°	2
Lat. N44°58'—Alt. 815'	8*	7*	8*	9*	12	12	9	9	9	8*		
Memphis	41°	44°	53°	62°	70°	78°	81°	80°	74°	64°	52°	4
Lat. N35°08'—Alt. 275'	11	10*	11	10	10	9	9	8	7	9		
Omaha	22°	26°	38°	52°	62°	72°	78°	75°	67°	55°	39°	2
Lat. N41°15'—Alt. 1040'	6*	6*	8*	10	12	11	9	9	8	7	5*	
Pittsburgh	31°	31°	40°	51°	62°	70°	74°	72°	67°	55°	43°	3
Lat. N40 26'—Alt. 745'	16*	14*	15*	13*	13	12	12	10	9	10	12*	1
St. Louis	32°	35°	45°	56°	66°	75°	80°	78°	71°	59°	46°	3
Lat. N38 37'—Alt. 455'	9*	9*	11*	11	12	11	8	8	8	8		

ROCKIES

	JAN.	FEB.	MAR.	APR.	MAY	JUNE	JULY	AUG.	SEPT.	OCT.	NOV.	DEC.
Denver	31°	33°	39°	48°	57°	67°	73°	71°	63°	52°	40°	3
Lat. N39 44'—Alt. 5280	5*	6*	8*	9*	10	8	9	9	6	6*	5*	
Salt Lake City	29°	34°	42°	50°	59°	68°	77°	75°	65°	53°	41°	3
Lat. N40 45'—Alt. 4390'	10*	10*	10*	9*	8	5	4	6	5	7	7*	1

SOUTH WEST

	JAN.	FEB.	MAR.	APR.	MAY	JUNE	JULY	AUG.	SEPT.	OCT.	NOV.	DEC.
Albuquerque	34°	41°	46°	54°	63°	73°	77°	74°	68°	57°	43°	3
Lat. N35 05'—Alt. 4950'	3*	3*	3*	4	4	3	8	8	5	4	2	
Phoenix	52°	56°	61°	68°	76°	85°	91°	89°	86°	71°	60°	5
Lat. N33 27'—Alt. 1090'	4	4	4	2	1	1	5	6	3	2	2	

WEST COAST

	JAN.	FEB.	MAR.	APR.	MAY	JUNE	JULY	AUG.	SEPT.	OCT.	NOV.	DEC.
Los Angeles	56°	56°	58°	60°	63°	67°	71°	72°	70°	66°	62°	57°
Lat. N34 03'—Alt. 340'	6	6	6	4	2	1	0	0	1	2	3	
Reno	32°	36°	42°		5°	63°	71°	69°	61°	51°	41°	34
Lat. N39 31'—Alt. 4490'	7*	6*				2	2	2	3			
San Francisco	50°		6°			59°	60°	62°	61°	57°	52°	
Lat. N37			0				0	2	4	7		
						45°	64°	60°	53°	46°	42°	
						8	5	8	13	17	16	

HOTELS
IN
GREAT BRITAIN
LES HÔTELS EN GRANDE BRETAGNE

THE · CLAVERLEY
ON · BEAUFORT · GARDENS

TRA27-02

TRA27-03

TRA27-09

TRA27-04   TRA27-10

TRA27-08

TRA27-05

TRA27-07

27 — TRA27-01   TRA27-06

TRA28-03

TRA28-04

TRA28-02

TRA28-05

TRA28-09

TRA28-08

TRA28-06

TRA28-07

TRA28-01   28

BRITISH
MAPS AND MAP-MAKERS

EDWARD LYNAM

COLLINS · 14 ST. JAMES'S PLACE · LONDON
MCMXLVII

Kiel, Bahnhof.

LEARN ONE THING
EVERY DAY

Golfo della

SPEZIA

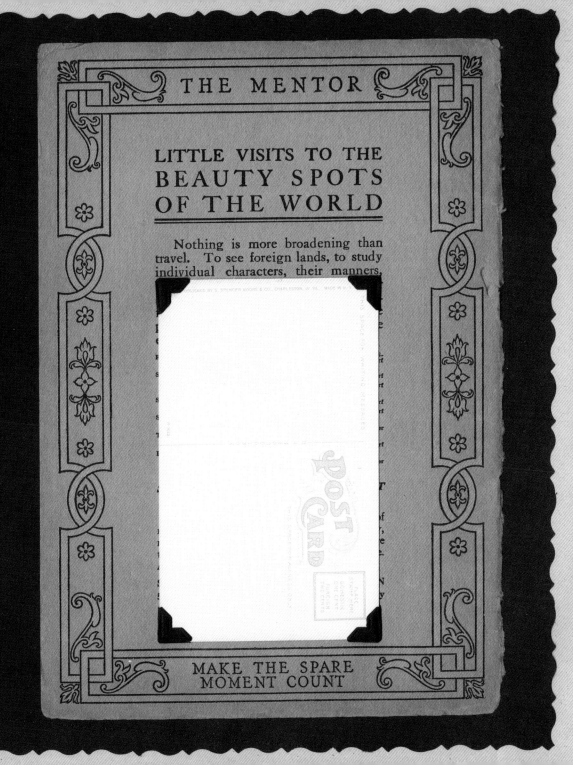

THE MENTOR

LITTLE VISITS TO THE BEAUTY SPOTS OF THE WORLD

Nothing is more broadening than travel. To see foreign lands, to study individual characters, their manners,

MAKE THE SPARE
MOMENT COUNT

TRA29-02

TRA29-03

TRA29-04

29 TRA29-01

TRA30-02

TRA30-03

TRA30-04

TRA30-05

TRA30-06

TRA30-07

TRA30-01 — **30**

DISTANCES BETWEEN THE LARGER CITIES
OF THE UNITED STATES

The distances are by the shortest usually traveled railroad routes. Compiled from the War Department's official table of distances.

FROM / To	New York	Chicago	Philadelphia	St. Louis	Boston	Baltimore	Cleveland	Buffalo	San Francisco	Pittsburg	Cincinnati	Milwaukee	New Orleans	Washington	Minneapolis
	Mls.	Mls.	Mls.	Mls.	Mls.	Mls.	Mls.	Mls.	Mls.	Mls.	Mls.	Mls.	Mls.	Mls.	Mls.
Albany	145	832	230	1,028	202	333	480	297	3,106	567	724	917	1,517	373	1,252
Atlanta	876	733	785	611	1,106	688	736	919	2,805	805	492	887	496	648	1,153
Baltimore	188	802	97	934	418		474	398	3,076	334	593	887	1,184	40	1,222
Boston	217	1,034	321	1,230		418	682	499	3,308	674	926	1,119	1,602	458	1,454
Buffalo	442	525	416	731	499	398	183		2,799	270	427	610	1,258	438	945
Chicago	912		821	284	1,034	802	357	520	2,572	468	296	85	912	820	420
Cincinnati	757	298	606	341	926	593	244	427	2,631	135		442	1,073	437	777
Cleveland	584	357	403	548	632	474	138	183	2,588	193	244	399	935	471	734
Columbus, O.	637	314	546	428	820	511	138	321	2,452	193	116	399	935	471	884
Denver	1,934	1,022	1,243	916	2,056	1,850	1,379	1,537	1,371	1,490	1,107	1,263	1,447	655	892
Detroit	693	272	669	488	750	649	172	251	2,588	921	263	357	1,092	1,269	163
Duluth	1,291	479	1,300	728	1,513	1,281	701	1,004	2,238	947	777	422	1,447	655	1,521
El Paso	2,310	1,452	2,219	1,245	2,414	2,179	1,703	1,915	1,287	1,866	1,556	1,550	1,165	2,130	1,521
Galveston	1,792	1,144	1,601	860	2,012	1,594	1,408	1,591	2,157	1,431	1,357	1,229	410	764	1,340
Grand Rapids, Mich.	821	178	815	462	878	790	332	379	2,452	462	308	263	1,090	553	508
Helena	2,452	1,540	2,361	1,549	2,574	2,342	1,897	2,065	1,250	2,008	1,838	1,455	2,152	2,320	1,119
Indianapolis	825	183	734	240	965	704	283	466	2,457	381	111	268	888	664	603
Jacksonville, Fla.	983	1,077	892	975	1,213	795	1,085	1,193	3,098	1,057	878	543	616	751	1,517
Kansas City	1,342	458	1,251	277	1,466	1,211	755	967	1,931	898	618	350	680	1,171	573
Los Angeles	3,149	2,265	3,058	2,084	3,273	3,018	2,563	2,774	475	2,705	2,425	2,350	2,007	2,978	2,301
Louisville	871	304	780	274	1,040	703	358	541	2,468	427	114	389	778	663	727
Memphis	1,157	527	1,006	311	1,287	939	738	921	2,439	807	494	612	396	929	894
Milwaukee	997	85	906	360	1,119	887	442	610	2,359	553	383		997	875	336
Minneapolis	1,332	420	1,241	586	1,454	1,222	777	945	2,096	888	718	335	1,255	1,210	
Mobile	1,231	929	1,140	647	1,461	1,043	1,029	1,212	2,623	1,038	826	926	141	1,003	1,233
Montreal	386	841	477	1,051	330	674	623	494	3,115	704	748	988	1,655	614	1,125
Newark, N. J.	76	903	82	1,056	226	179	575	405	3,177	635	833	1,363	1,363	219	1,323
New Haven	76	980	167	1,141	140	264	628	445	3,254	520	833	1,065	1,448	304	1,400
New Orleans	1,372	912	1,281	699	1,602	1,184	1,073	1,256	2,482	1,142	829	997		1,144	1,332
New York		912	91	1,065	217	188	554	442	3,186	444	757	997	1,372	228	1,332
Ogden	2,406	1,494	2,315	1,414	2,528	2,296	1,851	2,019	780	1,962	1,792	1,579	1,891	2,284	1,316
Omaha	1,405	493	1,314	413	1,527	1,295	817	1,018	1,781	961	791	578	1,080	1,283	381
Philadelphia	91	821		974	321	97	493	416	3,095	353	666	906	1,281	137	1,241
Pittsburg	444	468	353	621	674	334	135	270	2,742		313	853	1,142	302	883
Portland, Me.	332	1,149	436	1,345	115	533	797	614	3,423	789	1,041	1,234	1,717	573	1,569
Portland, Ore.	3,204	2,292	3,113	2,212	3,326	3,094	2,649	2,817	772	2,760	2,590	2,378	2,746	3,082	2,042
Providence	193	1,034	281	1,230	45	378	682	499	3,308	634	926	1,119	1,562	418	1,454
Quebec	530	1,013	621	1,343	402	718	795	612	3,287	876	1,039	1,038	1,827	786	1,433
Richmond, Va.	343	879	252	918	573	155	553	553	3,155	417	531	964	1,046	116	1,299
Rochester, N. Y.	373	603	361	799	430	354	251	68	2,877	338	495	658	1,324	394	1,023
St. Joseph, Mo.	1,392	470	1,301	327	1,474	1,261	875	1,058	1,807	948	668	555	941	1,221	485
St. Louis	1,065	284	974		1,230	934	548	731	2,194	621	341	369	699	894	586
St. Paul	1,322	410	1,231	576	1,444	1,212	767	935	2,086	878	708	326	1,275	1,200	10
San Antonio	1,943	1,204	1,852	920	2,150	1,755	1,468	1,651	1,911	1,581	1,217	1,389	571	1,715	1,320
San Francisco	3,186	2,274	3,095	2,194	3,308	3,076	2,631	2,799		2,742	2,572	2,359	2,482	3,064	2,096
Seattle	3,151	2,239	3,060	2,332	3,273	3,041	2,596	2,764	957	2,707	2,537	2,154	2,535	3,029	1,818
Spokane	2,812	1,900	2,721	1,932	2,934	2,702	2,257	2,425	1,205	2,368	2,198	1,815	2,600	1,479	1,479
Springfield, Mass.	139	935	230	1,131	99	327	583	400	3,209	583	891	1,053	1,394	967	1,385
Tampa, Fla.	1,195	1,309	1,104	1,187	1,425	1,007	1,297	1,405	3,310	1,269	261	203	329	595	1,729
Toledo	705	244	615	437	795	595	113	296	3,064	302	563	375	1,144		664
Washington	228	790	137	894	458	40	437	438							1,210

206. The North Walk, Indian Point. Hudson River

TRA31-04   TRA31-03   TRA31-02

TRA31-05

                                                                    TRA31-08

                    TRA31-06

31 —| TRA31-01 |

                                                    TRA31-07

TRA32-03

TRA32-02

TRA32-04

TRA32-05

TRA32-10

TRA32-06

TRA32-09

TRA32-07

TRA32-01 — 32

TRA32-08

Map of Connecticut, Page 265; Massachusetts, 107; New Jersey, 116; Pennsylvania, 124; Quebec, 73-75; Vermont, 131.

118

NEW YORK

Scale of Miles

C. S. Hammond & Co., N. Y.

105 AMERICAN FALLS FROM GOAT ISLAND, NIAGARA FALLS, N. Y.

MT. SHASTA, CALIFORNIA, ELEVATION 14,161 FEET   728

REPUBLICA DEL PARAGUAY 10 CENTIMOS

CORREOS DE COLOMBIA AEREO 30 CVS VOLCAN GALERAS - PASTO

223

TRA33-03　　　　　　　　　　　　　　　TRA33-02

TRA33-10

TRA33-09

TRA33-04

TRA33-08

TRA33-05

33 — TRA33-01　　　　　　　　　　　　　　　TRA33-07

TRA33-06

TRA34-03

TRA34-02

TRA34-04

TRA34-05

TRA34-06

TRA34-01 34

C-18—Royal Poinciana and Palm Trees, Palm Beach, Fla.

H. C. WIENEKE, IOWA CITY, IOWA

"C. T. ART-COLORTONE," MADE ONLY BY CURT TEICH & CO., INC., CHICAGO, U.S.A.

POST CARD

THIS SPACE FOR ADDRESS ONLY

TRA35-03   TRA35-02

                                    TRA35-08

TRA35-04

                                                TRA35-07

        TRA35-05

                        TRA35-06

— TRA35-01

TRA36-02

TRA36-03

TRA36-04

TRA36-01 36

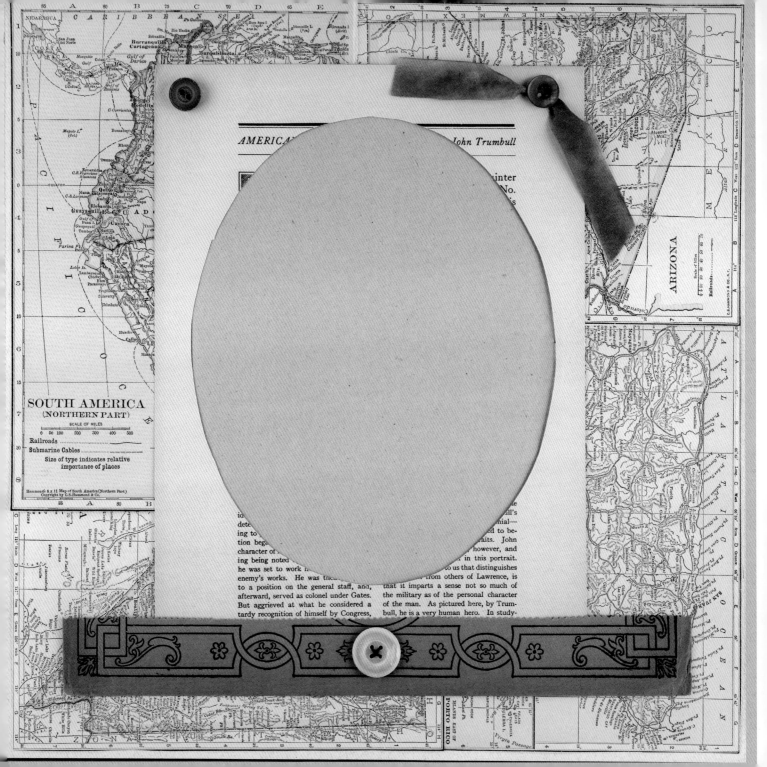

AMERICA... *John Trumbull*

...inter
... No.
...is

id...
dete...
ing to...
tion beg...
character of...
ing being noted...
he was set to work h...
enemy's works. He was the...
to a position on the general staff, and,
afterward, served as colonel under Gates.
But aggrieved at what he considered a
tardy recognition of himself by Congress,

...le
...ull's
...nial—
...d to be-
...aits. John
...however, and
... in this portrait.
to us that distinguishes
from others of Lawrence, is
that it imparts a sense not so much of
the military as of the personal character
of the man. As pictured here, by Trumbull, he is a very human hero. In study-

SOUTH AMERICA
(NORTHERN PART)
SCALE OF MILES
0 50 100   200   300   400   500
Railroads ....
Submarine Cables ....
Size of type indicates relative
importance of places

Hammond's 8 x 11 Map of South America (Northern Part)
Copyright by C.S.Hammond & Co.

ARIZONA

Scale of Miles
0 5 10 20 30 40 50 60 70
Railroads ....
C.S.HAMMOND & CO., N.Y.

In a pocket at the rear of the ch... ...ead was

THE UNITED STATES

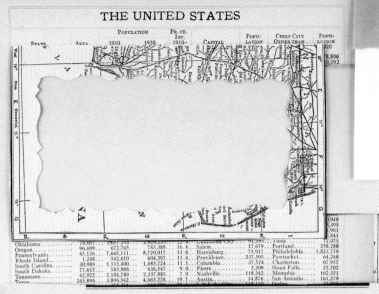

STATE	AREA	POPULATION 1910	1920	PR. CT. INC. 1910-	CAPITAL	POPU- LATION	CHIEF CITY OTHER THAN	POPU- LATION 1920
Oklahoma	70,057	1,657,155	2,028,283	22.4	Oklahoma City	91,295	Tulsa	258,288
Oregon	96,699	672,765	783,389	16.4	Salem	17,679	Portland	258,288
Pennsylvania	45,126	7,665,111	8,720,017	13.8	Harrisburg	75,917	Philadelphia	1,823,779
Rhode Island	1,248	542,610	604,397	11.4	Providence	237,595	Pawtucket	64,248
South Carolina	30,989	1,515,400	1,683,724	11.1	Columbia	37,524	Charleston	67,957
South Dakota	77,615	583,888	636,547	9.0	Pierre	3,209	Sioux Falls	25,202
Tennessee	42,022	2,184,789	2,337,885	7.0	Nashville	118,342	Memphis	162,351
Texas	265,896	3,896,542	4,663,228	19.7	Austin	34,876	San Antonio	161,379

AMERICAN MINIATURE PAINTERS *Lucia Fairchild Fuller*
SIX

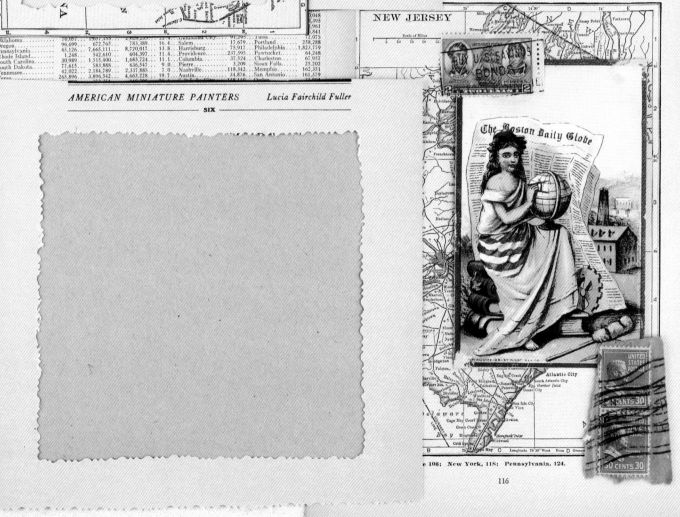

NEW JERSEY

The Boston Daily Globe

Atlantic City

...e 106; New York, 118; Pennsylvania, 124.

116

TRA37-03

TRA37-02

TRA37-04

TRA37-05

TRA37-06

TRA37-09

TRA37-07

TRA37-08

37 TRA37-01

TRA38-02

TRA38-03

TRA38-04

TRA38-07

TRA38-06

TRA38-05

TRA38-01 38

WESTERN PACIFIC

DATE | TIME | TRAIN ORDER

THE WESTERN PACIFIC RAILROAD COMPANY

OPERATORS' TRANSFER

UNITED STATES POSTAGE
FOUNDER OF THE
AMERICAN RED CROSS
CLARA BARTON
3¢

UNITED STATES POSTAGE
FOUNDER OF THE
AMERICAN RED CROSS
CLARA BARTON
3¢

Copyright, 1895, by Bryan, Taylor & Co.

NIGHT №

8
REX
AMSTERDAM
BROOM CO.
AMSTERDAM N.Y.

COMING ON DUTY | GOING OFF DUTY | STATION
SIGNATURES OF OPERATORS
OPERATOR | REMARKS

DATE	TIME	TRAIN ORDERS — SPECIFY EACH BY ITS NUMBER	Messages	TO WHOM ADDRESSED	OVERDUE TRAINS	SIGNATURES OF OPERATORS — OPERATOR RELIEVING	OPERATOR RELIEVED	ARKS
1940 Aug. 26th	4:00 P.m	228			1st 561			
		247		In Resompe for Exa 321 West	2nd 561			
		235			3rd 561			

ADMIT ONE

352092

352092

INDIANA TICKET CO.

DAY №

211

calling
ked in
f a sil-
hat had
er had
c under
led to
om his

a girl's
"But,
e of it
and I,
n above
e came
he was
rld. I
rful to
e loved
resting

F

SOUTH UNION STATION, DEWEY SQUARE, BOSTON, MASS.

TRA39-02

TRA39-07

TRA39-03

TRA39-06

TRA39-04

TRA39-05

TRA39-01

TRA40-02

TRA40-03

TRA40-04

TRA40-10 TRA40-09

TRA40-05

TRA40-06 TRA40-08

TRA40-07

TRA40-01 **40**

HUDSON

POST CARD

THIS SPACE FOR ADDRESS ONLY

PLACE
DOMESTIC
ONE CENT
FOREIGN
TWO CENTS
STAMP

THIS SPACE FOR WRITING MESSAGES

PLACE
ONE CENT
STAMP
HERE
MADE IN U. S. A.

POST CARD

PUBLISHED BY WOODCOCK'S DRUG STORES, COEUR D'ALENE, IDAHO

"TICHNOR QUALITY VIEWS" REG. U. S. PAT. OFF. MADE ONLY BY TICHNOR BROS., INC., BOSTON, MASS.

75415

THIS SPACE FOR WRITING MESSAGES.   R-7732

POST CARD

THIS SPACE FOR ADDRESS ONLY.

144

CORREOS DE COLOMBIA

III CENTENARIO DEL COLEGIO MAYOR
DE NUESTRA SEÑORA DEL ROSARIO-BOGOTA
1653   1953

FRAY CRISTOBAL DE TORRES
FUNDADOR

10   CENTAVOS   10

ATLANTIC SOUTHWESTERN BROOM CO. BALTIMORE, MD.

⑥ ATLANTIC

ATLANTIC

THE RIDE INTO LIFE   289

cision, the planning how and when to take that

71479   A SEA URCHIN

TRA41-02

TRA41-03

TRA41-04

TRA41-11

TRA41-10

TRA41-05

TRA41-09

TRA41-08

TRA41-06

TRA41-07

41 — TRA41-01

TRA42-03

TRA42-02

TRA42-04

TRA42-07

TRA42-05

TRA42-06

| TRA42-01 | 42 |

PLAYING THE GAME   191

SALT
from
Great
Salt Lake
Utah

411   PORTION OF SALTAIR PAVILION ON GREAT SALT LAKE, SALT LAKE CITY, UTAH

119414

455 A. GARDS HOUSE, SALT LAKE CITY

NORTH

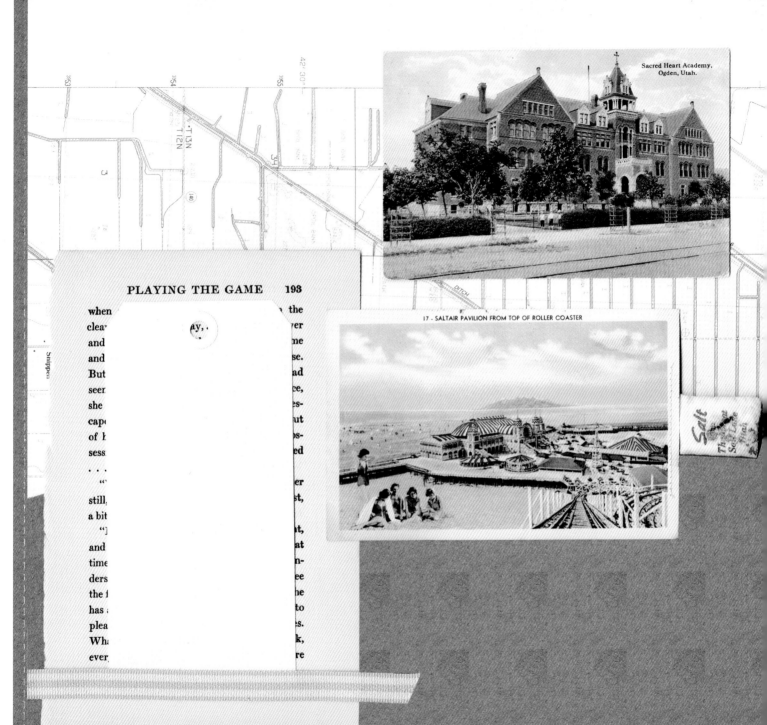

Sacred Heart Academy,
Ogden, Utah.

17 - SALTAIR PAVILION FROM TOP OF ROLLER COASTER

TRA43-02

TRA43-03

TRA43-07

TRA43-04

TRA43-06

TRA43-01

TRA43-05

TRA44-03   TRA44-02

TRA44-04

TRA44-05

TRA44-06   TRA44-07

TRA44-09

TRA44-01 — **44**

TRA44-08

ROUTE MAPS

ROADS · MILEAGE
HIGHWAY NUMBERS

FROM _San Francisco, Calif_

VIA

TO _Mt Shasta City Calif St Office (M R W)_

ISSUED BY

DATE _6-3-40._

CALIFORNIA STATE AUTOMOBILE ASSOCIATION

HEADQUARTERS: 150 VAN NESS AVENUE
SAN FRANCISCO, CALIFORNIA

Form 529

MAP SERVICE
OF THE
AUTOMOBILE CLUB OF SOUTHERN
CALIFORNIA
FIGUEROA AT ADAMS ST – LOS ANGELES

SAN
BERNARDINO   REDLANDS
Garage-Hotel

COLTON   LOMA LINDA

BEAUMONT

BANNING
Garage-Hotel

EL CASCO

RIVERSIDE

AUTOMOBILE ROAD MAP
FROM
SAN BERNARDINO
TO
IDYLLWILD AND RETURN

SCALE IN MILES

COPYRIGHTED BY THE
AUTOMOBILE CLUB OF SO. CALIFORNIA

18

AVERAGE FAHRENHEIT TEMPERATURES
+ DAYS OF RAIN
FOR CITIES IN THE UNITED STATES
TO COMPARE WITH OTHER COUNTRIES

EAST

	JAN.	FEB.	MAR.	APR.	MAY	JUNE	JULY	AUG.	SEPT.	OCT.	NOV.	DEC.
Boston	29°	29°	37°	47°	58°	67°	72°	70°	64°	54°	43°	32°
Lat. N42°21'—Alt. 21'	12*	10*	12*	11*	11	10	10	10	9	9	10*	11*
New York	31°	31°	39°	49°	60°	69°	74°	73°	67°	56°	45°	35°
Lat. N40°45'—Alt. 55'	12*	10*	11*	11	11	11	11	10	9	9	9	11*
Portland, Maine	20°	22°	33°	43°	53°	62°	68°	67°	59°	50°	38°	25°
Lat. N43°39'—Alt. 160'	12*	11*	13*	11*	12	12	11	10	10	10	11*	11*
Washington, D. C.	35°	36°	44°	54°	65°	73°	77°	75°	69°	57°	46°	37°
Lat. N38°53'—Alt. 25'	11*	10*	12*	11	12	11	11	11	8	8	9	10*

SOUTH

EXPENSE RECORD

DATE	TOWN	ITEM	COST	MILEAGE

TRA45-02

TRA45-03

TRA45-07

TRA45-06

TRA45-04

TRA45-05

45 ── TRA45-01

TRA46-03

TRA46-02

TRA46-04

TRA46-08

TRA46-05

TRA46-07

TRA46-06

TRA46-01 | 46

DETAILS..

SHUFFLEBOARD COURTS, LAKE WORTH, FLORIDA

Map of Asia, Pages 44-45.

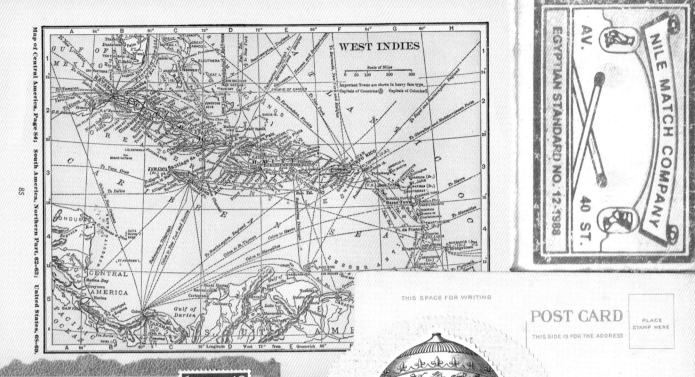

Map of Central America, Page 84; South America, Northern Part, 62-63; United States, 65-69.

85

WEST INDIES

Bilhete Carta

senh.

Francisco Nascimento

Largo da Conceição 4

Setúbal

VIA AÉREA
PAR AVION · PORTUGAL

HELVETIA 10
NÄFELS

THIS SPACE FOR WRITING

POST CARD

PLACE STAMP HERE

THIS SIDE IS FOR THE ADDRESS

EGYPTIAN STANDARD NO. 12-1988

AV. 40 ST.

NILE MATCH COMPANY

TRA47-02

TRA47-03

TRA47-04

TRA47-08

TRA47-09

TRA47-07

TRA47-05

TRA47-06

47 — TRA47-01

TRA48-02

TRA48-03

TRA48-04

TRA48-09

TRA48-05

TRA48-06

TRA48-08

TRA48-07

TRA48-01 48

Pennsylvania Turnpike and Lincoln Highway
through the Narrows. West of Everett, Pa.

SB-72—West Cabrillo Boulevard and Municipal Swimming Pool, Santa Barbara, California

ACME

-No 9-

Hamburg Broom Works.
Hamburg, Pa.

TRA49-02

TRA49-03

TRA49-04

TRA49-08

TRA49-05

TRA49-07

49 — TRA49-01

TRA49-06

TRA50-02

TRA50-03

TRA50-04

TRA50-05

TRA50-01   50

TRA51-02

TRA51-03

TRA51-04

TRA51-05

TRA52-02

TRA52-03

TRA52-04

TRA52-05

TRA52-09   TRA52-08

TRA52-07

TRA52-06

TRA52-01   52

A New & Exact
MAP
OF THE ISLAND OF
BARBADOES
IN *AMERICA*

According to an Actual & Accurate Survey

Made by William Mayo;

Approved by the ROYAL SOCIETY *& Authorized*

BY HIS MAJESTY'S ROYAL LICENCE

A Scale of *English* Statute Miles.

Hawaiian Postage 13 13½ Cents.

Hawaiian Postage 5 Five cents.

CARTOUCHE ON ... BARBADOS, 1722
By courtesy ... *ritish Museum*

MADE IN EGYPT

OCEANIA AND THE PACIFIC
ON MERCATORS PROJECTION

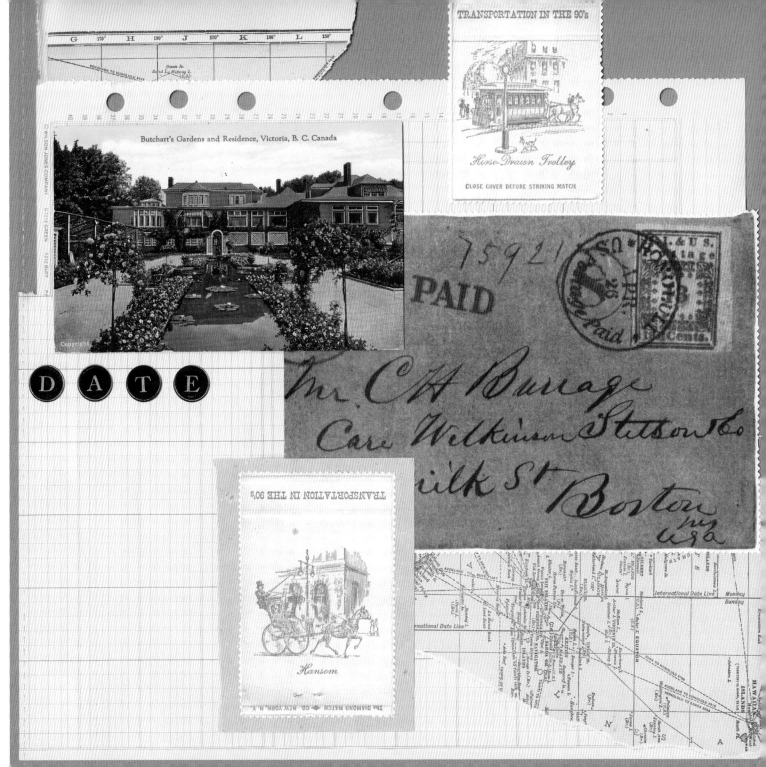

TRANSPORTATION IN THE 90's

Horse-Drawn Trolley

CLOSE COVER BEFORE STRIKING MATCH

Butchart's Gardens and Residence, Victoria, B. C. Canada

© WILSON JONES COMPANY

G-7212 GREEN   7212 BUFF

DATE

75921

PAID

Mr. CH Burrage
Care Wilkinson Stetson Co
Milk St Boston
Mass
USA

TRANSPORTATION IN THE 90's

Hansom

The Diamond Match Co. New York, N.Y.

International Date Line   Monday
Sunday

HAWAIIAN
ISLANDS

G 170° H 180° J 170° K 160° L 150°

TRA53-02

TRA53-03

TRA53-04

TRA53-11

TRA53-05

TRA53-10

TRA53-09

TRA53-08

TRA53-06

TRA53-07

 TRA53-01

TRA54-02

TRA54-03

TRA54-09

TRA54-04

TRA54-08

TRA54-07

TRA54-05

TRA54-06

TRA54-01 **54**

The Tower of Tōji, Kyoto.　京都東寺五重の塔

富貴
廣東吉祥公科司造

长城饭店
The Great Wall Hotel
Beijing

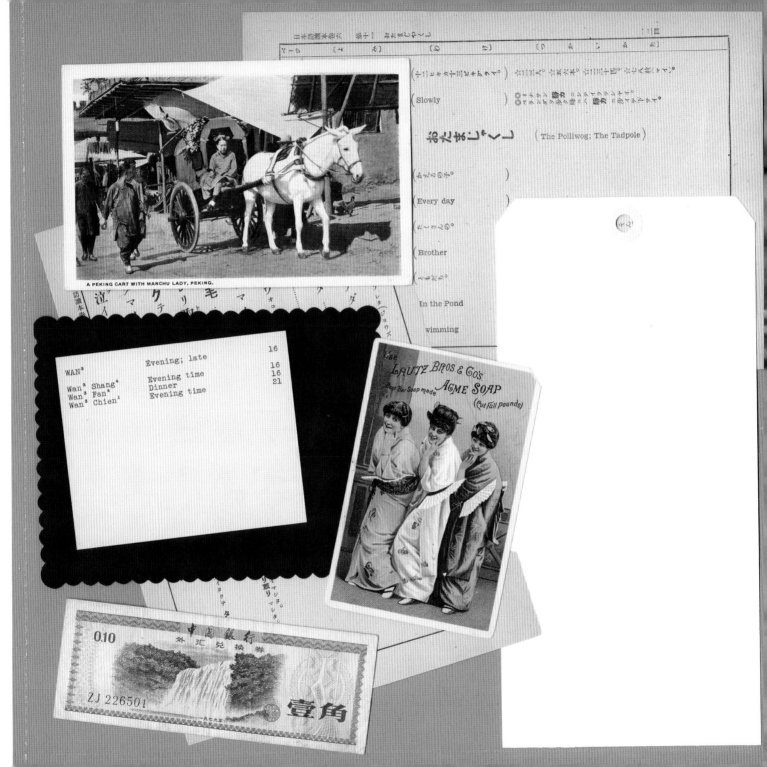

A PEKING CART WITH MANCHU LADY, PEKING.

(Slowly

(The Polliwog; The Tadpole)

Every day

Brother

In the Pond

Swimming

WAN³	Evening; late	16
	Evening time	16
Wan³ Shang⁴	Dinner	16
Wan³ Fan⁴	Evening time	21
Wan³ Chien¹		

Use LAUTZ BROS & CO'S
Best Bar Soap made ACME SOAP
(Cut full pounds)

0.10
中國銀行
外匯兌換券
ZJ 226501
壹角

TRA55-02

TRA55-03

TRA55-04

TRA55-09

TRA55-08

TRA55-07

TRA55-06

TRA55-01

TRA55-05

TRA56-03

TRA56-02

TRA56-04

TRA56-07

TRA56-05

TRA56-06

TRA56-01 56

TRA57-03

TRA57-02

TRA57-04

TRA57-09

TRA57-08

TRA57-05

TRA57-06

57 TRA57-01

TRA57-07

☆始メ
（ハジメ）

..... Begin
☆ミンナデ話ヲ始メマシタ。

（ヤカマシクサワイデ
　ガヤ〳〵ユウ。）
☆ハチガヘヤノ中ニスッテ來タノデ、ミンナガ **大サワギ**シマシタ。

（タイヘンサワグコト）
Does not move
☆ジットオ日様テミツメテイルト、目ガ見エナクナリマス。

（ヨクミテ。）
◎オトウトハヨクフトッテイマス。**シカシ**私ヨリモチカラガヨワイ。

（ダガ、ケレドモ。）
☆大ゼイノ子供ガ **ドン〳〵**走ッテ行ク。サア〳〵皆サン **ドン〳〵**オハイリナサイ。

（ズン〳〵）
Next; Another
☆ニイサンハ、ケサハ **大急**ギデ學校ヘ行キマシタ。

（タイソウイソイデ。）